1 85103 046 8

First published 1986 by Editions Gallimard
First published 1988 in Great Britain by Moonlight Publishing Ltd,
131 Kensington Church Street, London W8
© 1986 by Editions Gallimard
English text © 1988 by Moonlight Publishing Ltd

THE BOOK OF RIVERS

DISCOVERERS

Written by Genevieve Dumaine
Illustrated by Brigitte Paris

Adapted and translated by Penny Stanley-Baker

MOONLIGHT PUBLISHING

Contents

The water cycle	**8**
From mountain spring to mighty river	**10**
Rivers in myth and legend	**12**
The Ganges	**14**
Rivers in art	**16**
Running water meets hard rock	**18**
The rush and tumble of the mountain torrent	**20**
Salmon, dauntless riders of the rapids	**22**
Otters and beavers	**24**
Fishing and fish farming	**26**
The full and fertile middle course	**28**
Waterfalls and dams	**30**
Migratory fish	**32**
Floating forests	**34**
Riches of the river-bed	**35**
The Nile	**36**
The lowland river	**38**
Long boats and tall boats and all sorts of craft	**40**
Canals: man-made waterways	**42**
The Mae Nam Chao Phraya	**44**
Bridges: more than just a way across	**46**
Crafts and industry	**48**
Fertile floods and irrigation	**50**
Journey's end: the river mouth	**52**
Arctic rivers	**54**
The Amazon	**56**
Rotterdam: Europe's greatest river port	**58**
Pollution	**60**
What is an ecosystem?	**62**
Adapting to a life in the water	**64**
Rare creatures of the river	**66**
A source of energy that will never run dry	**69**
An A to Z of river facts	**70**
About the author and the illustrator	**75**
Places to go and story-books to read	**76**

The water cycle

1. Water falls as snow, hail, rain, etc.
2. Watershed
3. Catchment area, comprising river basin
4. River system
5. Upland stream
6. Upper course
7. Middle course
8. Confluence
9. Tributary
10. Water-mill and mill race
11. Spring
12. Reservoir
13. Hydro-electric dam
14. Fish farm
15. Lower course
16. Canal lock
17. Barge
18. Towpath
19. Nuclear power station
20. Sewage farm
21. Suspension bridge
22. Estuary
23. Fishing grounds with dipping nets
24. River port
25. Delta
26. Evaporation and cloud formation

From mountain spring to mighty river

In limestone areas, water wears away the limestone rock, carving out great caves through which the river flows underground, to emerge elsewhere as a spring (like this limestone stream on the flanks of Pen-y-Ghent in the Pennines).

The Niagara Falls

A river is water running on its way down to the sea. All rivers begin life on high ground.

Where does the water come from? When rain falls, some soaks into the ground and collects under the surface. This is ground water. The rest, running away over the surface, is called sheetwash. Ground water,

The hydra thrives in fast-flowing water.

sheetwash and melting snow form rivers.

The first stage in the river's journey to the sea is its upper course. The water is flowing in a fast, concentrated stream, wearing down the rock, eroding a channel. It displaces and carries with it earth, stones, even rocks. Few plants or animals are equipped to survive in the swirling current which threatens to sweep them away. On leaving the steep slopes, the river enters its middle course. It slackens in pace as other streams flow into it, and it becomes wider. In its calmer waters, many forms of plant and animal life thrive.

Away, you rolling river...

Black American Spiritual

In its lower course, the river is flowing over much flatter ground. It is deeper and more sluggish as it meanders towards the sea. Some of the material displaced in the upper course is deposited as silt in the bends of the river. River banks and flood plains support an abundance of animal and plant life.

In Nigeria, it is the women's task to fetch water from the river.

Many rivers are the favourite haunts of holiday-makers in their pleasure boats.

At the river mouth, where the river meets the sea, the flow slows right down. Often the river forms a delta, a marshy area of low islands and mud flats alternately uncovered and covered by the ebb and flow of the tide. Deltas are home to a great variety of animals and plants, both freshwater and marine.

The course of a river moulds the landscape through which it flows. Rivers supply many of our most basic needs: water, food, energy, transport.

Cattle go down to the river to drink.

Rivers in myth and legend

China bowl of the Sung dynasty

In Germanic legend, sirens haunted river estuaries, enticing sailors to their doom with their singing.

These carved wooden statues represent sick people who, in Gallo-Roman times, sought healing at this holy spring.

The great rivers of the world have always inspired a mixture of fear and respect. Men recognized in them a life-giving force of nature which was fundamental to the progress of civilization. They were often worshipped as gods.

People associated the ceaseless flow of the river and the constant renewing of its waters with the return of spring and the process of regeneration, which are represented in China by the dragon.

From the earliest times, rivers were considered places of healing. The river Ganges is still held sacred by the people of India today.

In legend as in life, rivers were nonetheless also linked with death. The Romans believed that there were four rivers which the souls of the dead must cross before they could enter the Underworld. In Ancient Egypt, the river Nile was the boundary between the world of the living to the East and the world of the dead to the West.

In Ancient Egypt, funeral barges carried the souls of the dead across the Nile.

Charon, the bearded ferryman of Greek and Roman mythology, transported the spirits of the dead across the four rivers of the Underworld, the Acheron, the Styx, the Cocytus and the Phlegethon.

In Benin, the Yorubas worship the river-goddess Oshun.

From his temple near the first cataract, the god Khnum, with his ram's head, was said to watch over the sources of the Nile. With his foot, he held back the floodwaters.

13

The Ganges

Each day, as the sun rises, holy men spend hours in prayer on the banks of the Bhagirathi river.

Beranese

The Ganges has a catchment area three times the size of the British Isles. Its waters irrigate the heavily populated plain through which it flows and are crucial to the survival of the inhabitants.

The Ganges ensures the fertility of the land. It is sacred to all Hindus, who believe that bathing in its waters purifies the soul.

The Ganges has its course in the Himalayas. It is fed by two main tributaries, the Bhagirathi, which rises in an icy cave 6 000 metres up, known as the 'Mouth of the Cow', and the Alaknanda, which rises in Tibet.

By the time it reaches Beranese, the Ganges has become a mighty river. It fans out over a wide river-bed, flanked on either side by high banks, and dotted with islands.

Near the Bay of Bengal, the waters of the Ganges and Brahmaputra combine to form an arm of sea, a 'sound', which is over 100 kilometres wide in some places. The level of the Ganges remains fairly constant, although, at certain times of year, melting snow and the summer monsoons can cause it to rise up to 10 metres.

For 350 million Hindus, the Ganges is a fundamental part of their way of life and their religion. The most sacred places of pilgrimage in India are found along its banks.

In Beranese, the banks of the Ganges are lined with flights of marble steps 25 kilometres long and 40 metres high. These are the famous 'Ghats', down which people walk to bathe in the waters of the river. According to Hindu belief, the souls of those who die in Beranese are freed from further reincarnations.

In India, the bodies of the dead are burned. Their ashes are scattered over the water of the Ganges.

Pilgrims' offerings are carried away downstream.

Ganga Mai, Mother Ganges, flows out of Shiva's hair or Vishnu's feet. Her waters wash away all the sins of mankind.

Rivers in art

Aboriginal bark-painting of a freshwater fish

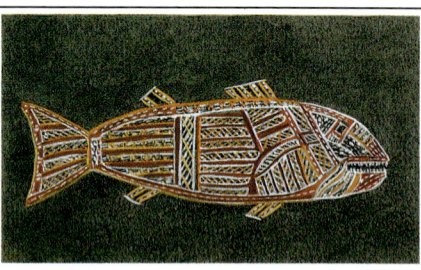

Throughout the centuries, the running water which the river carries from its spring high in the mountains, over the plains and out to sea, has been a source of inspiration to painters, writers, sculptors and poets alike.

*Dear, I know nothing of
Either, but when I try to imagine a
faultless love,
Or the life to come, what I hear is the
murmur
Of underground streams, what I see is
a limestone landscape.* (W.H. Auden)

Silver ornament depicting a Celtic river-god

A Roman mosaic from Tripoli

But rivers are not only sustaining and life-giving; they also carry with them the power to kill, to devastate and to destroy.

Haulage of heavy goods. Gallo-Roman bas-relief.

Coat of arms of the city of Paris.

The constantly changing nature of the river is often used to portray the constant changes of life itself.

Statue of the River Tiber from the Four Rivers Fountain in Rome

The château of Chenonceaux in the Loire valley in France

Running water meets hard rock

Erosion is when a hard substance is worn down, until gradually, over a long time, it has been completely ground down and transformed. Running water is the most powerful eroding agent there is. Rivers are constantly wearing away their beds and depositing rocks and earth.

The strength of the current is determined by the slope or gradient. As the gradient decreases, the river begins to erode sideways, widening its course. It also begins to drop some of the lightest sediment. Gradually, these deposits accumulate on the river-bed, raising it above the level of the surrounding valley floor. The river tends to overflow its banks.

As the ground over which the river flows gets flatter, the river follows the lie of the land more. Wherever it encounters an obstacle, it changes direction slightly, forming bends or meanders. The river deposits material on the inside of the bend, but eats into the outside. Sometimes, when the river changes course, it leaves behind a crescent-shaped bend, known as an ox-bow lake.

The current slackens further as the river nears the sea. Rocks and stones, pebbles and gravel, sand and mud are deposited to form an alluvial plain.

Some rivers can cut down deep into hard rock, forming entrenched meanders. The most spectacular example is the Grand Canyon in the United States, where the Colorado river has cut through layer upon layer of rock over millions of years.

When the river is low, parts of the river bed are exposed.

The course of every river is determined by the geological composition of the soil over which it flows; some rocks, like limestone, wear away much more quickly than hard rocks, like granite. The climate, how hot it is, how much rain falls, and what sort of plants grow in and beside the river all affect the way it develops too.

How to recognize the age of a river by the shape of its valley:

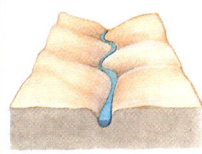

1. Steep-sided gorge: young river

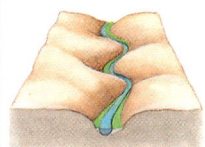

2. Widening river-bed, alluvial deposits: mature river

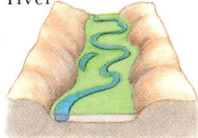

3. Gentle slopes: ageing river

4. Flood plain: old river

The rush and tumble of the mountain torrent

Animals and plants have to adapt to their turbulent habitat. They are streamlined to offer as little resistance as possible to the current. Insects tend to be flat, with strong legs fringed with hair to carry them through the water. Plants have long green fronds which drift with the current.

All upland streams have their source in the mountains. A huge sort of funnel, known as the catchment area, channels ground water, sheetwash and melting snows into a single watercourse. Pieces of stone and branches prised loose by the water can get caught in the narrow, winding gorge. As the rushing water spins them round and round, they wear away the sides and bottom to form potholes, or 'giant's kettles'. It is not so much the water but the material it carries with it that does the eroding. Much of this material is deposited at the foot of the steepest slope, forming a sort of minidelta or alluvial fan.

Mountain streams often form cascades. The current is strong, the water clear, shallow and well-oxygenated. In the rush and tumble of the torrent, survival depends on being able to hold fast. Moss and algae attach themselves to rock; the larvae of certain winged insects, leeches and worms are all equipped with suction pads or hooks with which they can anchor themselves to a rock or stone.

Trout, minnows, bullhead, loach and river lampreys live in mountain streams. The musk rat and the water shrew hunt their waters and make their holes in the steep banks.

Salmon, dauntless riders of the rapids

Salmon ladder with pools

Salmon ladder with baffles

Salmon lift for high dams

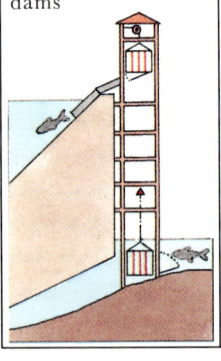

Salmon live in the sea, but spawn in rivers. In late autumn, the female salmon make their way upstream from the sea to the gravelly spawning grounds, where they lay their eggs.

In the following spring, the salmon fry hatch. The young fish grow quickly, and are soon swimming around in shoals. They are now called parr.

By the time they are 2 years old, the salmon are 12 to 18 centimetres long and silvery-grey. They are now ready to begin their long migration downstream to the sea. They face upstream and allow the current to carry them down tail-first.

When they reach the estuary, they pause long enough to acclimatize themselves to the salt water. Then they swim out to sea, where they spend the next 4 years feeding on small salt-water fish and shellfish.

It is then time for them to return to their birthplace. The journey is long and arduous. They have to swim against the current all the way, covering distances of 30 to 100 kilometres a day.

The scent of the home stream leads the salmon back to where they hatched. There they spawn. Great numbers die of exhaustion.

Wherever dams have been built in salmon rivers, special salmon ladders or lifts are set up so that the salmon can still make their way up the river.

River pollution puts salmon at risk. Many of today's salmon are raised on special farms in Scandinavia, Scotland and Canada.

Salmon farm

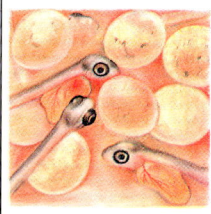

In water at 2°C, salmon fry will hatch within 200 days.

How do salmon leap up waterfalls? They grip their tails in their mouths and let go suddenly, so that their bodies uncoil like taut springs.

Otters and beavers

Otters are expert swimmers. They catch unsuspecting fish by diving down and coming up underneath them.

Otters are members of the weasel family. They can move swiftly and silently on dry land, preferring to venture out of the water under cover of darkness. Male otters may travel long distances over land in search of a mate. Yet the otter is even more at home in the water. It can see perfectly underwater. When it swims, using its webbed feet and long tail to steer with, it can twist and turn as lithely as an eel. In cloudy water, it uses its long whiskers to locate fish and shellfish on the river-bed.

At the top of the next page you can see a beaver's lodge:
1. Dam
2. Pool made by beavers
3. Underwater entrance
4. Living quarters
5. Ventilation shaft
6. River

The beaver, too, is amphibious. Beavers are found only in the Northern Hemisphere, where they live in colonies on rivers where there are plenty of trees. The American beaver is larger than the European beaver.

The beaver is a rodent. It gnaws through young trees and saplings with its strong front teeth.

Beavers build dams to create quiet pools in which to swim and fish. They build a complex network of waterways and canals so that they can float the logs they need for their dams to where they want them.

A beaver's lodge is a hive of activity. Beavers live in family groups of as many as 12 members. Young beavers, or kits, stay with their parents for about 2 years, after which the adults force them out to make room for younger brothers and sisters.

Beavers are now in danger of becoming extinct.

Fishing and fish farming

In countries where food is scarce, much of the protein in people's diet is supplied by freshwater fish. Fishing is a vital industry. However, in countries where food is plentiful, fishing is often a hobby or sport. Of all the fish eaten in the world, a quarter are freshwater fish.

There are many ways to catch fish, most requiring skill and patience. Some of the more unusual methods are quite spectacular.

Line fishing is a popular sport

Fishermen of the Wagenia tribe

In the Congo, the Wagenia fishermen sling logs together to make a sort of scaffolding across the rapids. From this structure they suspend large baskets which they direct into the current.

At the height of the dry season in Nigeria, when the river Sokoto is low, fish collect in pools. The Hausa go after them, taking triangular nets fitted with large empty gourds to keep them afloat.

The idea of raising fish is not a new one. The first fish farms were in China, where carp were raised over 2 500 years ago. In the Middle Ages in Europe, monasteries had carp ponds so that the monks could have fresh fish all the year round.

There are two methods of fish farming. The fish are either left in their natural environment, but protected so that they increase in number, or raised intensively, in artificial tanks.

Fish farming on a Norwegian river

This Amazonian Indian aims to one side of the fish to allow for the distortion of the water.

Hausa fishermen

The full and fertile middle course

Somewhere on its way down to the plain, the stream becomes a river. It is broader now and flows more steadily, with many an eddy and waterfall along the way. Shallows and rapids develop where the ground rises, and deep pools form wherever there is a dip in the river-bed. The current is no longer strong enough to carry anything but sand and gravel. Larger stones are deposited in the form of shingle.

The water is still clear, but warmer and less highly oxygenated than in the mountain stream. The mixture of sand and shingle on the river-bed allows a few floating plants, such as water-lilies, to take root. In the summer months, the water level drops, exposing parts of the river-bed. Grayling and chub frequent this stretch of the river. Salmon travel upstream to spawn on the gravelly river-bed.

Willows and poplars line the grassy river banks, where kingfishers and many water animals make their homes. Wild flowers take root in the firm soil, untroubled by floods.

The minnow reach:

The deeper waters of the river's middle course are home to many crustaceans, amongst them the crayfish. Crayfish are about 15 cm long and look like small lobsters. They are greenish or brown in colour. They hide under stones during the day and are active at night, using their large pincers to catch food. Fish such as minnows and salmon feed on the crustaceans. These fish in turn attract birds such as kingfishers to the river banks.

White wagtail

Waterfalls and dams

Above: the Beni Isgen dam in Algeria gives water for irrigation.
Below: in South America, the Itaipu dam provides hydro-electricity.

Wherever a river flows over hard rock on to softer rock, the soft rock is eroded more quickly and a waterfall forms. This may be anything from rapids, where water gathers momentum and is dangerous to navigate, to the most spectacular of waterfalls.

Negotiating the rapids of the river Congo in a dugout canoe

A dam is a barrier built across a river to control its flow. Its chief functions are to hold floodwaters in check, and to store water in the lake or reservoir created behind it. This water can then be diverted to adjacent land or forced through turbines to create electricity. Meanwhile, enough water is released from the dam to maintain fish and other wildlife further downstream.

Dams help preserve farmland from the erosion caused when rivers flood their valleys.

Leaping the falls in a kayak

The Angel Falls in Venezuela are the highest in the world.

Migratory fish

An adult eel may be 1.5 m in length and weigh as much as 4 kg by the time it migrates.

Some fish leave their natural habitat to lay their eggs. Sturgeon, lampreys, shad and salmon all travel up-river from the sea in order to spawn. What causes fish to migrate is not known. It is probably a natural instinct to reproduce where the young will have the best chances of survival.

Leptocephalic larva   Elver

The eel

The eel larva hatches at a depth of about 400 metres in the Sargasso Sea, and spends 2 years drifting with the current before reaching land and moving up-river as an elver. It is 10 years before the eel, fully grown, journeys down the river to make its way out to sea, and back across the Atlantic to its birthplace. There it spawns and dies.

Many of the Atlantic currents converge in the Sargasso Sea, where eels go to spawn.

The sturgeon

With its long snout and bony plates, the sturgeon is unmistakable. It lives in coastal waters at a depth of about 200 metres. When it is about 10 years old, it finds the mouth of the river and swims upstream to spawn in the upper reaches. Not long after they hatch, the

sturgeon fry head downstream towards the sea.

The sea lamprey

Lampreys are parasitic, and suck the blood of other fish in the coastal waters where they live. The seven holes on either side of their rubbery bodies are their gills.

In spring, the adults travel up-river to spawn. Two weeks later, the lamprey larvae hatch. It is some years before they return to the sea.

The shad

An increasingly rare member of the herring family, it lives at sea. In the spring, the adult fish migrate up-river.

Young sturgeon are raised to restock the river. When they are caught, fishermen ring them and put them back in the river.

The sea lamprey fastens on to its victim using its sucking disc, and drains its blood.

Between April and June, shad are fished at sea using trammel nets.

Floating forests

In parts of Asia, elephants are used to carry the timber to the river.

In forested areas, rivers are an ideal means of transporting timber downstream to the sawmills and papermills.

In the fast-flowing reaches of the river, lumberjacks stand astride the lengths of timber using long poles to stop the logs piling up and to steer them in the right direction. In the lower reaches of big rivers, the trunks are bound together with chains and long trains of them are pulled by tugs.

Riches of the river-bed

Alluvium is sediment deposited by a river. Small boulders and pebbles, the most bulky materials, are deposited first as shingle. Many rivers have shingle beds in their upper reaches. Smaller stones are worn down into gravel and deposited further downstream. Silt, sand and clay, often rich in organic matter and yielding fertile soil, are deposited last.

Gold nuggets in a panning tray

Rivers provide not only rich soil, but also building materials such as gravel, sand and mud.

Sometimes alluvial deposits contain gold. Gold is extracted by drilling underground shafts and galleries, but it is also mined in the river-bed itself. The gold-bearing sand and gravel are placed in panning trays and rinsed repeatedly. The gold nuggets or gold powder, being heavier, stay in the trays as the lighter materials are washed away.

Much of the world's tin ore is found in alluvial form, as are platinum and some gem stones.

Enthusiasts still pan for gold in many rivers in Europe.

Panning for gold in Finland

35

The Nile

Isis, the Ancient Egyptian goddess, mourned her husband Osiris. Where her tears fell, there rose the Nile.

The river Nile is over 6 700 kilometres long. It winds its way from its source through equatorial, then tropical regions and finally through the desert before flowing out into the Mediterranean at its delta in Egypt.

The Blue Nile Falls in Ethiopia

The water-wheel moves water from the river to irrigation channels.

Before the Aswan dam was built, the floods spread fertile silt over the surrounding countryside.

The Nile is fed by two main tributaries, the White Nile and the Blue Nile. The headwaters of the White Nile rise in Burundi and flow on into the Sudan in a succession of waterfalls and swamps. The Blue Nile rises in the mountains of Ethiopia. It is the rain falling in these mountains which caused the Nile to flood each year. The two rivers converge at Khartoum in the Sudan to form the main river Nile.

Now, Lake Nasser, the largest artificial lake in the world, lies upstream of the Aswan dam.

The lowland river

As a river enters the final stages of its journey, it is flowing over flatter ground. Swollen by tributaries, it winds its way much more slowly towards the sea, fanning out over a wide bed, where it deposits silt and alluvium. The flows of the lowland river is often controlled by dams and locks.

The gently flowing, warmer, often muddy waters of the lowland river are

A warning to boaters and bathers:

The shallower water along the banks may appear to be scarcely moving, but beware! The current can be very strong nearer the middle of a river.

Blue damselflies mating

home to carp, bream, tench, eels and sturgeon. There is a plentiful supply of worms, insects and molluscs for them to feed on in the accumulated mud and silt of the river-bed. The sand and lush vegetation of the river banks are rich feeding grounds for a great variety of animal life.

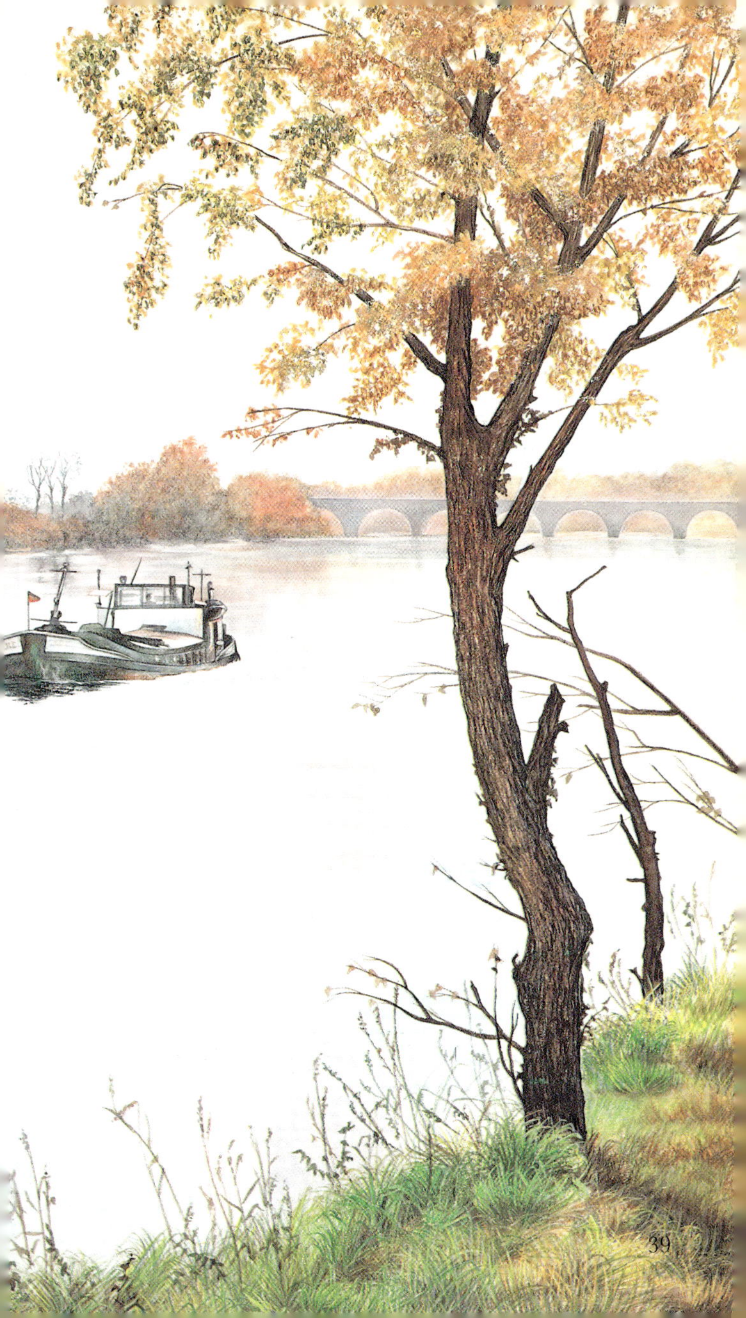

Long boats and tall boats and all sorts of craft

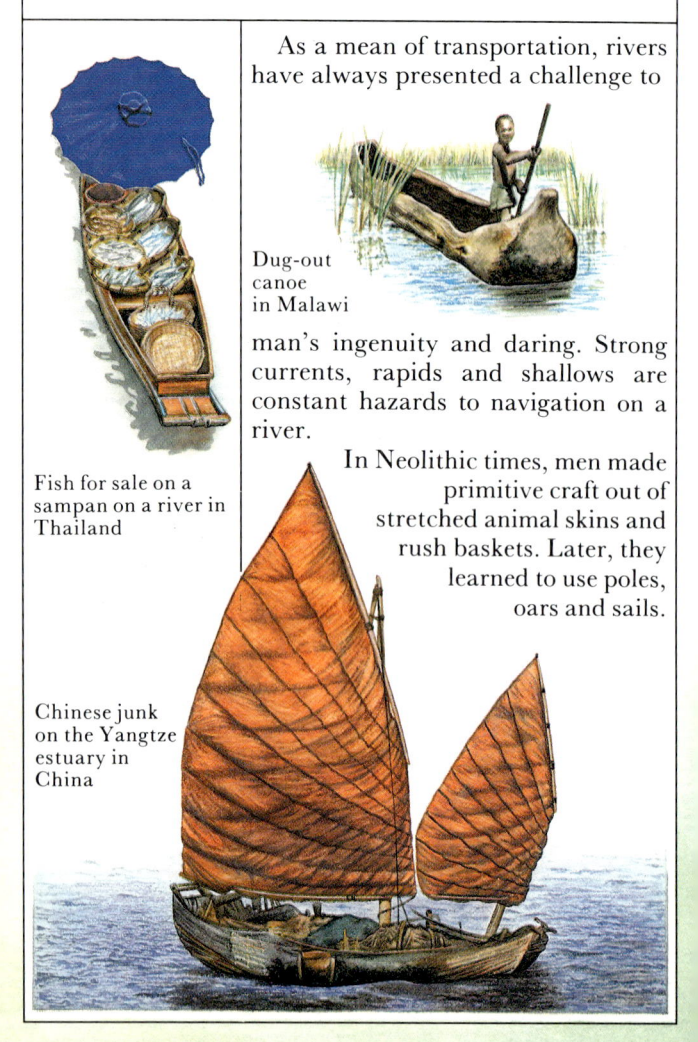

As a mean of transportation, rivers have always presented a challenge to

Dug-out canoe in Malawi

man's ingenuity and daring. Strong currents, rapids and shallows are constant hazards to navigation on a river.

In Neolithic times, men made primitive craft out of stretched animal skins and rush baskets. Later, they learned to use poles, oars and sails.

Fish for sale on a sampan on a river in Thailand

Chinese junk on the Yangtze estuary in China

Mississippi paddle-steamer

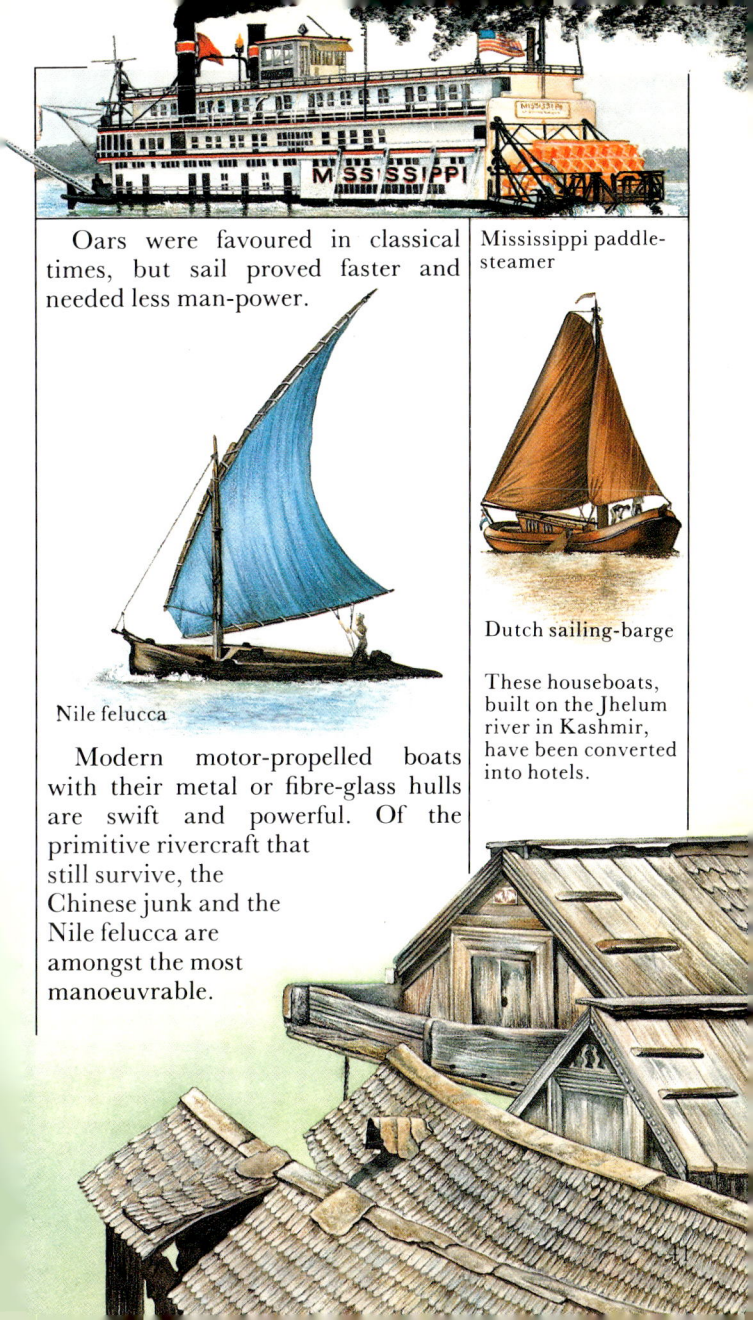

Oars were favoured in classical times, but sail proved faster and needed less man-power.

Nile felucca

Modern motor-propelled boats with their metal or fibre-glass hulls are swift and powerful. Of the primitive rivercraft that still survive, the Chinese junk and the Nile felucca are amongst the most manoeuvrable.

Dutch sailing-barge

These houseboats, built on the Jhelum river in Kashmir, have been converted into hotels.

Canals: man-made waterways

The first canal in the world was dug in the thirteenth century. But the great age of canal-building was the nineteenth century, at the height of the Industrial Revolution, when coal and other heavy freight needed to be moved swiftly and cheaply.

Networks of canals were first built to allow heavy goods to be transported by boat. Some canals provide a link between one river and another, others link one sea to another, like the Suez and the Panama canals, and others link a town to the sea, like the Manchester Ship Canal.

Many of the older canals still in existence today are not wide enough to take boats of more than 280 tonnes. Others, however, have been built more recently, using modern techniques, and will carry huge barges up to 1350 tonnes. These are mostly used to transport coal, iron, oil, gravel, sand and grain.

Canal du Midi, linking the Mediterranean to the Bay of Biscay

During the Industrial Revolution, a great network of canals grew up in Britain, linking the major industrial areas of the north-west and of the Midlands with London and the Thames, Severn, Mersey and Trent rivers. With the increasing use of the railways many canals fell into disuse.

All early barges had to be towed, by men or by horses.

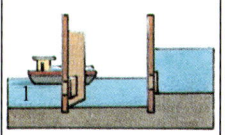

1. Tail bay

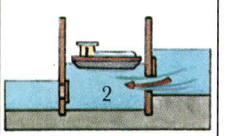

2. Lock basin

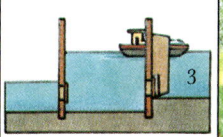

3. Head bay

Going upstream, the boat enters the lock from the tail bay. The watertight gate closes. Water is let in from the head bay until the level in the lock is equal to that in the head bay. The head bay gate opens and the boat proceeds upstream.

43

The Mae Nam Chao Phraya

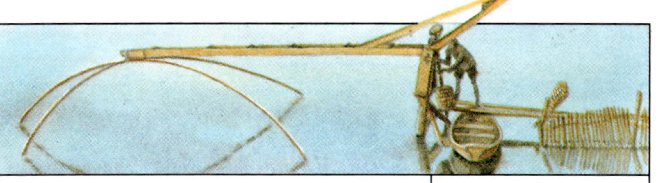

In Thailand and in most of Southeast Asia, rivers are not just a means of communication or transportation, they are a way of life. The entire population lives either on the water or along the banks. The jumble of houses is built on stilts, so close together that you can step from one to the next. Many people actually live on board the little flat-bottomed boats or sampans that thread their way in and out of the houses. They scarcely ever need to set foot on dry ground. Markets are held on the water.

The river supplies drinking water for both people and livestock, water for domestic needs, for drainage and for the irrigation of paddy-fields.

Fishing in the middle of the river using a drop net.

The water hyacinth grows in profusion where the water is slow-moving.

The Mae Nam Chao Phraya is Thailand's busiest and most useful river system.

The Royal Pavilion at Bang Pa In

45

Bridges: more than just a way across

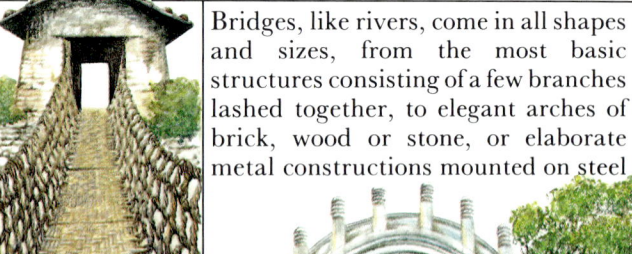

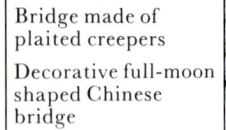

Bridges, like rivers, come in all shapes and sizes, from the most basic structures consisting of a few branches lashed together, to elegant arches of brick, wood or stone, or elaborate metal constructions mounted on steel girders. Some are functional, others are decorative, the best are both. Some of the most exciting metal bridges were designed by the brilliant nineteenth century British engineer, Brunel.

Bridge made of plaited creepers

Decorative full-moon shaped Chinese bridge

Enclosed timber bridge, New England

Even in ancient times, men were familiar with the basic principles of bridge-building. Nowadays, the use of iron and steel means that the distances spanned are much greater.

Some bridges are designed to move. There are three sorts of movable bridge. A swing span bridge is supported by a central pier on which the bridge pivots in a semi-circle, allowing boats to pass on either side. On a bascule bridge, the bridge divides in two: each half can be raised in order to let traffic through. On a vertical lift bridge, however, the roadway remains horizontal, and is raised and lowered in one piece. Many bridges have a specific function: viaducts carry rail or road traffic; aqueducts carry water; canal bridges carry river traffic.

In France, a canal-bridge carries the Canal du Midi over the river Orb.

Tower Bridge in London is a bascule bridge.

The Pont du Gard in southern France

Crafts and industry

Water is an essential element in the preparation of certain products, such as wool, leather, paper and sheet metal, all of which require prolonged soaking in water. High-quality paper and sheet metals both need to be steeped in soft water.

A Persian carpet being washed in stream water near Tehran. The carpet makers maintain that the minerals in the water bring out the brightness of the colours.

De-liming hides in a tannery

In England, the early textile industry grew up in remote rural areas in the north which were well-served by clear rivers and streams.

Tanning is the process by which hides are made into leather. All tanneries used to be near rivers. The soaking and softening of the hides, first in water and then in lime, together with the scraping of the outer skin and hair, used all to be done in the river itself.

Hydro-electric power is produced from heavy turbines within the power station. What happens is this: water stored in the lake flows down pipes on to the blades of a turbine, making it turn round and round at high speed. The shaft of the turbine is connected to a generator which produces electricity. Inside the generator is a copper coil which spins round, activated by the turbine, in a magnetic field. This is what creates the electricity.

At the French tidal power station in La Rance, the water power is supplied not by an artificial lake, but by the ebb and flow of the tide. This station is unique.

The tidal power station at La Rance

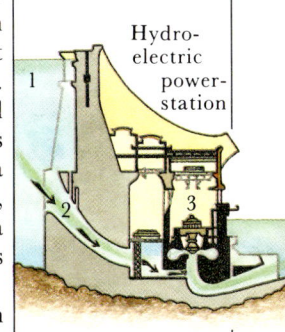

Hydro-electric power-station

1. Head of water
2. Pipeline
3. Turbine

A nuclear power station drawing water from a nearby river.

Fertile floods and irrigation

Not a single drop of water falling on this island shall find its way to the ocean without having first been put to good use by mankind.

Extract from a 12th century Sri Lankan water conservation programme

Thanks to irrigation, three rice crops can be grown in a single year.

Floods can alter the character of a river-bed dramatically. They may erode the banks and existing bends, so causing the river to change course.

Rivers flowing across plains and tropical rivers are particularly prone to seasonal flooding. When the river floods its banks, it deposits a layer of fertile silt on the surrounding land.

Floods need not be disastrous. Without the regular flooding of the Nile, the soil of Egypt would not have been rich and fertile. Nowadays, floodwaters and flooding can often be predicted.

At Guilin in China, irrigation in the paddy-fields helps to preserve the plant life of the uncultivated upland areas.

One-eighth of all the land under cultivation in the world is irrigated. As a result, the productivity of existing fertile land has increased and much previously unproductive land is now used for growing crops.

In all irrigation schemes, the contents of river water are carefully analysed. For example, in desert areas, where evaporation is intense, an excess of salt can damage the soil. Another danger is the spread of infectious disease through contaminated water.

Palm trees line the banks of the wadi in flood.

Canal irrigation system used by the Incas

Each strip of land is surrounded by water on three sides.

Water is still transferred from the Nile into irrigation ditches by means of the ancient shadoof.

Journey's end: the river mouth

On the Guadalquivir delta in Spain, a purple heron wades through the reeds as greater flamingoes wheel and turn overhead. Open stretches of salt-water marshes are havens for birds.

Estuaries and deltas are the places where fresh water and salt water meet.

Many river mouths were formed 6000 years ago when, as the glacial ice melted, the sea level rose and flooded low-lying valleys.

Three main types of river mouth are easily distinguishable:

– a ria is the mouth of a fjord. These steep-sided glacial valleys evolved very little over time. The water is deep where it meets the sea;

– an estuary is a wide, flat area where alluvial deposits accumulate;

– a delta is where the sediment deposited fans out into the sea.

In certain conditions, an exceptionally high tide can actually reverse the flow of the river, sending the water back upstream in a vast tidal wave.

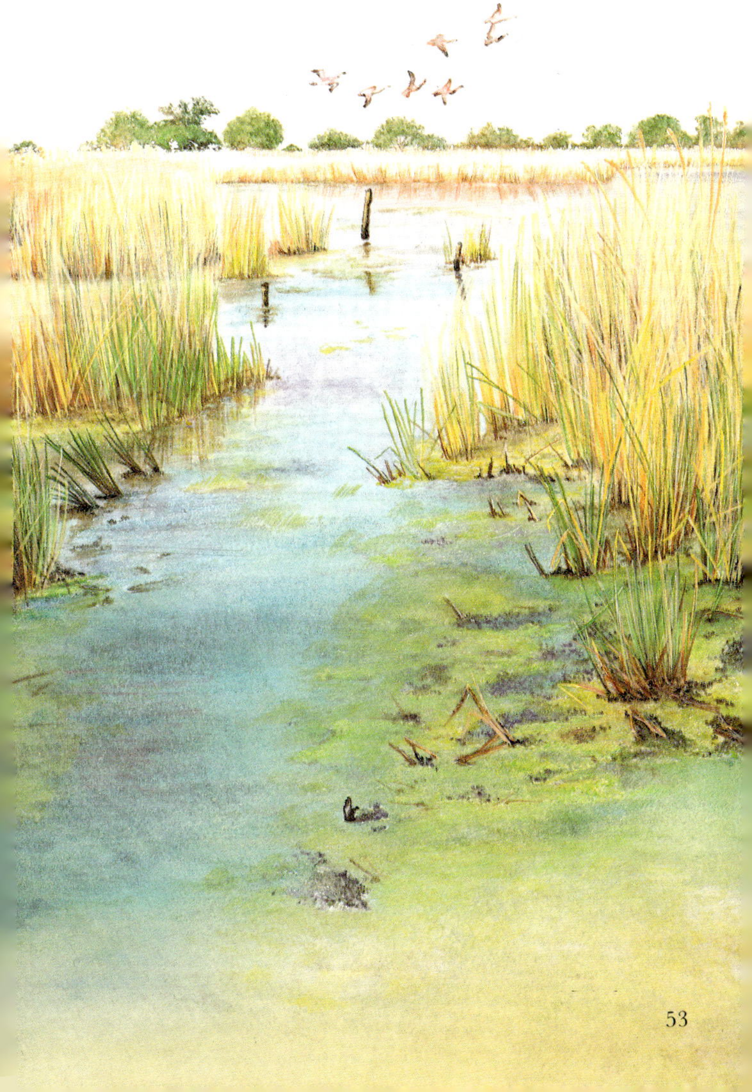

Arctic rivers

The American elk, the largest member of the deer family, feeds on lichen.

Brown bears prove to be expert at catching fish when salmon are migrating.

The barnacle goose returns to Alaska each year to nest.

These rivers are freed from the grip of the Arctic ice for only a few months of each year.

The largest and most typical of the polar rivers are the Mackenzie in America, and the Ob, the Yenisey and the Lena in Siberia. Each of these rivers is over 5000 kilometres long and flows into the Atlantic Ocean.

The catchment area of these polar rivers is covered in ice and snow for 8 months of the year. These so-called permafrost conditions are what determine the marshy vegetation of the Tundra. In their lower course, the rivers are often very wide.

The polar rivers are fed by the melting of the snow in the spring and by the summer rains. In May or June, the thick crust of ice covering the river begins to crack and break up into great blocks of ice, which jolt and jostle their way ever faster downstream. As the snows melt, the river swells and bursts its banks. The long winter is over.

Eggs and seeds and hibernating animals, which have lain dormant throughout the winter months, all suddenly come to life. The migrating birds return. Summer has come to the cold North.

The Mackenzie delta

On many of the rivers in Alaska, the ice never melts completely.

As soon as the snow melts, sphagnum mosses appear.

Lichens survive beneath the heavy covering of snow.

In summer, the deltas are covered in wisps of Arctic cotton grass.

The Amazon

Piranha; a shoal of piranhas can devour a large animal in a matter of minutes.

A familiar scene in the suburbs of Manaus in Brazil.

Many of the backwaters of the Amazon are covered in the huge leaves of the giant water-lily.

The Amazon is over 6500 kilometres long. The Amazon basin is a vast network of over a thousand rivers and tributaries. They comprise more than two-thirds of the world's supply of fresh water. The Amazon rises in Peru, 5000 metres up in the Andes, and flows rapidly down to the Brazilian plain in a series of waterfalls and rapids.

Two main tributaries, the muddy yellow Rio Solimões, and the peaty black Rio Negro, run parallel for a distance of 80 kilometres before converging to form the Amazon itself.

As the land levels out, the Amazon flows on into a vast area of marshy, equatorial forest.

The only way through the dense Amazonian forest is by boat. Large ships can sail up the Amazon as far as Iquitos (about 3600 kilometres).

The volume of water flowing out of the Amazon into the sea each day is as much as or more than the volume that flows out of the Thames, the Rhine or the Seine in a whole year. So vast is the mass of water passing out to sea that the salt water is pushed back over a distance of 160 kilometres.

At the equinoxes, the turning of the tide creates an immense tidal wave which the Indians call the 'great roaring'.

The Amazon forest is home to thousands of different animals and plants. There are more species of fish in the Amazon than in all the other rivers of the world put together. These unique riches are now under serious threat from the destruction of the rain forests.

Scarlet ibises make their homes amongst the exposed roots of a mangrove swamp.

The Anavilhanas Archipelago of the Rio Negro consists of a tangled string of interconnected islands.

Rotterdam: Europe's greatest river port

The Euromaast with its rotating observation platform towers above the city and port. Built in 1960, it was raised a further metre in height in 1970 to 105 m.

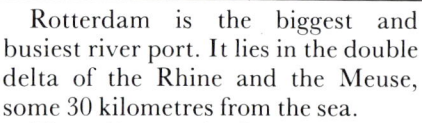

Rotterdam is the biggest and busiest river port. It lies in the double delta of the Rhine and the Meuse, some 30 kilometres from the sea.

The Port of Rotterdam, or Europoort (Europort), as it is called, can accommodate the largest ocean-going vessels, including oil-tankers of 200 000 and 400 000 tonnes.

Much of the cargo passing through the port is oil, but other heavy goods such as coal, minerals and grain are also handled. In Rotterdam, cargoes are off-loaded from sea-going vessels on to the barges that will take them to their destination by river.

The Rhine The great German river, the Rhine, is an international waterway, where navigation is free of charge and customs duty. It provides access to a network of canals and rivers serving Switzerland, France and Germany, amongst them the Meuse, Moselle, Elba, Neckar and Danube.

Certain sections of the Rhine presented natural obstacles to navigation in the form of shallows, rapids and pronounced meanders. In places, the course of the river has been straightened, canalized, dug out, or even diverted to form a parallel canal (the Alsace Grand Canal). Work is now under way to connect the network of rivers and canals to that of the Rhône.

The Rhône is one of the busiest freight-carrying rivers in France.

The central European network connects Austria, Belgium, Bulgaria, Czechoslovakia, East Germany, France and Hungary with the Netherlands, Poland, Romania, Switzerland, the Soviet Union, West Germany and Yugoslavia.

Rotterdam is a free port, where goods exported and imported are not subject to customs duty. Many processing industries have grown up in the port. Raw materials can be brought in, processed and shipped out duty-free.

Low, flat barges towed by tugs are used to carry heavy cargoes such as gravel.

Pollution

Rivers are used as dustbins. Domestic waste is one of the main causes of pollution.

The Mississippi river, the 'Father of Waters', as it was known by the Indians, is one of the great rivers of the world. Sadly, it is now heavily polluted.

Our modern industrial society produces more and more waste: human and animal waste, and the toxic chemicals from factories. Much of this finds its way into our rivers and waterways.

Many fish and birds fall victim to pollution.

The use of large quantities of fertilizers, pesticides and weedkillers in modern farming means that high concentrations of these harmful substances end up in our rivers. As the quality of the water deteriorates, so the animal and plant life dependent on it suffers or is destroyed.

Nowadays, scientists determine what pollutants are present in the water by carrying out a careful study of the animal community. This method of water analysis is based on a biological principle: species sensitive to pollutants will die out, while resistant species increase in number.

Worldwide efforts are being made to reduce the extent of pollution. Much dirty water is now recycled in special water treatment plants before being returned to the river or sea.

There are four stages in this purification process:
– solids are eliminated from the water;
– harmful bacteria are removed;
– toxic chemical substances such as nitrates and phosphates are removed;
– the water is filtered, and the acidity level is corrected.

Many of the solids resulting from this can be processed and recycled in the form of fertilizers, but not all.

Water hyacinths attract toxic chemical and metal elements in the water.

The disease bilharziasis is transmitted by a worm which lives in a freshwater snail. In Africa, the disease has spread rapidly because of the number of irrigation channels where the snails breed.

Blindness or onchoceriasis, caused by minute worms, is transmitted through the bites of little flies, simulids, which live in running water in the tropics.

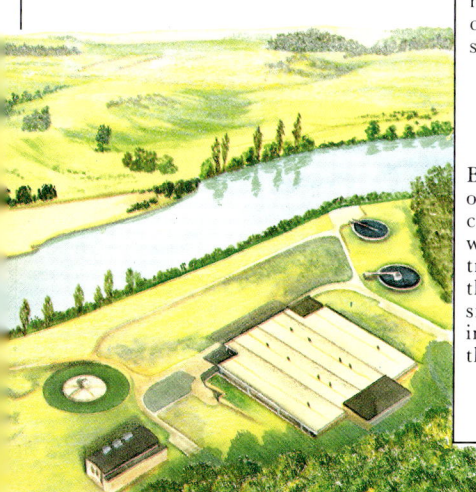

What is an ecosystem?

The plants and animals living in a particular environment, together with the physical and chemical factors that make up that environment are what we call an ecosystem.

Rivers can be divided into different zones according to the amounts of light, temperature, oxygen and minerals they contain.

In Europe, the different river zones are:

– the trout zone, where the water is clear, cold and turbulent;
– the grayling zone, highly oxygenated;
– the barbel zone, with substantial variations in temperature and numerous species;
– the bream zone, conditions similar to pond life, water rich in organic matter;
– the flounder zone, the estuary, where the water is salty and the current changes with the tide.

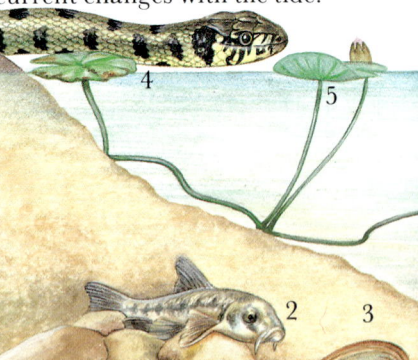

River zones:

Trout (zone 1) very fast-flowing current 2 m per second; highly oxygenated: from 10 to 8 cm^3 per litre, from 5 to 10°C

Grayling (zone 2) fast-flowing current: 0.5 to 1 m/s; oxygen 8 to 7 cm^3/l, from 8 to 14°C

Barbel (zone 3) moderately fast flow: 0.25 to 0.5 m/s; oxygen 7 to 6 cm^3/l, 12 to 18°C

Bream (zone 4) slow-moving; 0.10 to 0.25 m/s; oxygen 6 to 5 cm^3/l, 16 to 20°C

| Zone 1 | Zone 2-3 | Zone 4 | Zone 5 |

An ecosystem is a recognizable self-contained habitat. Broadly speaking, zones 1 and 2 correspond to the upper and middle stretches, 3 and 4 to the lowland stretches, and zone 5 to the estuary.

Bulrushes

1. Crayfish
2. Gudgeon
3. Freshwater mussel
4. Water snake
5. Water-lilies
6. Dipper
7. Damselfly larva
8. Water snails
9. Water shrew
10. Frog
11. Waterskater
12. Horsetail
13. Newt
14. Freshwater shrimp

River-bank plants:

Marsh marigolds grow in profusion in the water-meadows of the river plain.

Butterbur is found by fast-flowing streams.

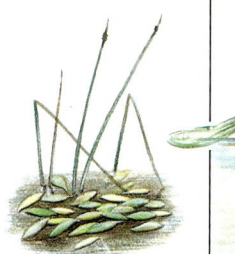

Reeds and waterspike are features of pond and marsh.

Adapting to a life in the water

Aquatic species are well-adapted to life in or on the water.

The frog, the crocodile and the hippopotamus have eyes and nostrils strategically placed near the tops of their heads so that they can see and breathe as they glide through the water.

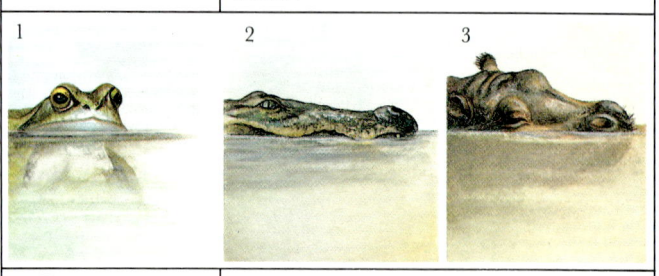

1. Frog
2. Crocodile
3. Hippopotamus

Surprisingly, some fish can even catch their food out of the water. The archer-fish catches insects it sees perched on a reed or grassy verge out of the water by dislodging them with a spray of water. The catfish uses its long whiskery barbels to rake the muddy river-bed for grubs.

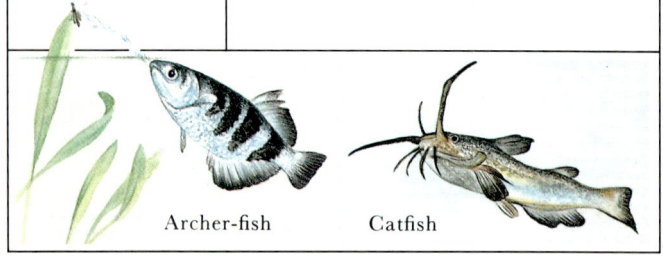

Archer-fish   Catfish

The flamingo sifts out grubs and insects from the cloudy water with a comb-like filter in its bill.

In fast-flowing streams, insect larvae encase themselves in little open-ended tubes made of sand grains, twigs and leaves, which resist the tug of the current.

Greater flamingo
Duck

Caddis fly larva in its case

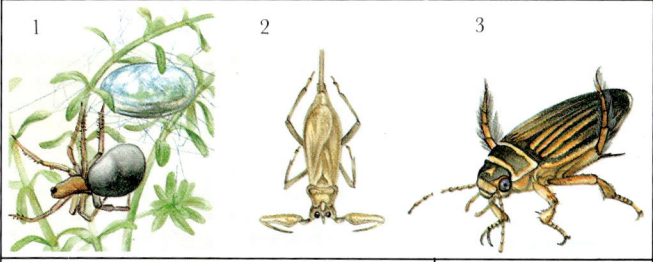

1 2 3

Some insects spend their lives in the water, but still need to breathe air. The water spider (1) spins an underwater net, which it fills with air like a diving bell. This is its home.

The water scorpion (2) has a long siphon like a diver's schnorkel which it pushes up out of the water in order to breathe.

The great diving beetle (3) rises regularly to the surface in order to breathe through its tail.

The jacana, or lily-trotter, uses its extremely long toes to step across floating water-lily leaves.

Jacanas are found on marshes or slow-moving rivers in the tropics.

Rare creatures of the river

The gentle manatees of Florida may have been taken for mermaids in the past.

The pink Amazonian dolphin can find its way through even the cloudiest water using ultrasound.

Spadefish 6 m long have been found in the Yangtze river in China.

Manatees

Manatees can grow up to 4 metres in length. These harmless herbivores can consume up to 50 kilogrammes of water plants in a day. In Florida, they are now a protected species.

Freshwater dolphins

Unlike other dolphins, they can move their heads independently of their bodies.

Mudskippers

These curious pop-eyed fish live in shoals in the tropical mudflats of Africa, Asia and Australia. The largest species have suckers on their fins, which enable them to move out of the water, periodically flipping upright on to their tails, rather like sea-lions. Some can climb vertical shoots using their sucker-fins.

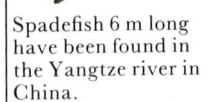

Spadefish

Like its close relative the sturgeon, the spadefish used to be fished for its roe. It is now increasingly rare.

The duck-billed platypus

With its streamlined body, rubbery bill and webbed feet, this curious mammal is ideally suited to conditions on the river-bed. It can stay under water for up to 5 minutes at a time, and protects itself by means of a poisonous spur on its hind leg.

Another animal in danger of extinction is the spectacled cayman of the Amazon basin

Capybaras

The biggest of all the rodent family, these giant guinea-pigs have webbed feet and strong claws. Capybaras are excellent swimmers and can stay under water for long spells.

The duck-billed platypus is a very unusual mammal. It lays eggs and suckles its young.

The Pyrenean desman is a member of the mole family, which has survived unchanged since the Tertiary era. It feeds on larvae in the cold, fast-flowing streams of the Pyrenees, where pollution is threatening to make it extinct.

Capybara

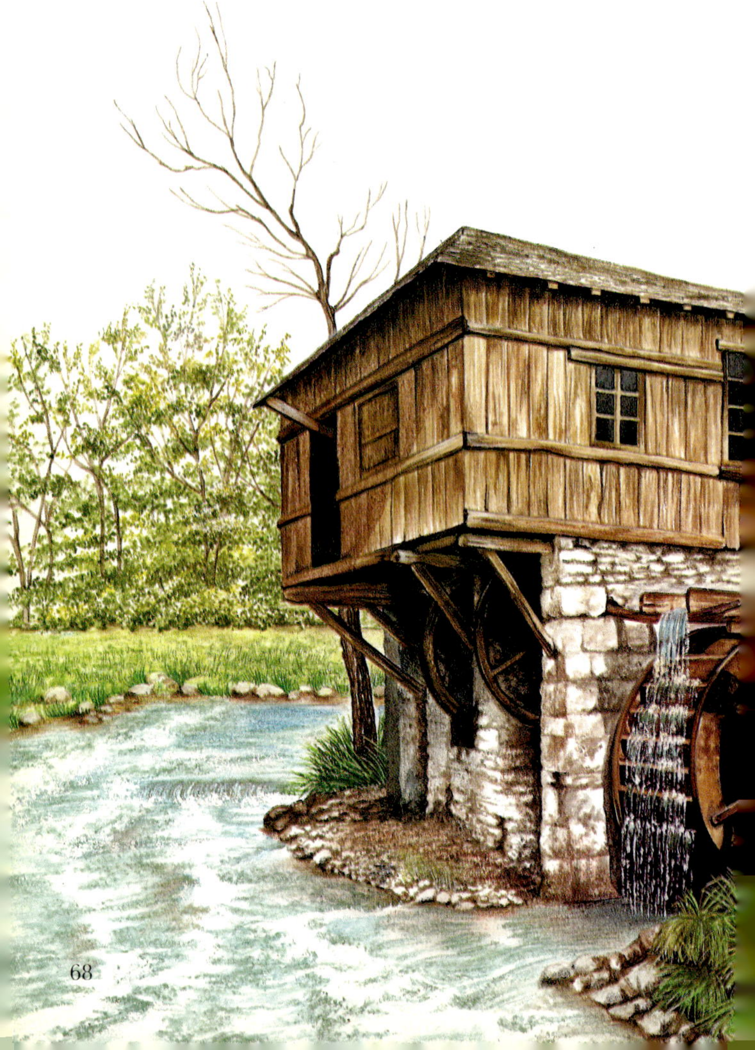

A source of energy that will never run dry

Early in history, men found ways of harnessing the power of running water. In the first century B.C., the Romans were using water-wheels connected to grinding stones to mill grain.

A water-wheel converts the energy of falling water into mechanical energy. Primitive water-wheels were mounted on frames over a river. The flowing water striking the blades caused the wheel to turn. In more sophisticated versions of the water-wheel, such as the one you see here, the water is directed on to the wheel from on top by means of a chute.

The wheel was mounted on an axle, which was linked either to a millstone or to machinery. Water-mills were usually built near waterfalls or rapids where the river was fast-flowing.

Before the invention of the steam engine, water was a major source of energy and many factories depended on water power.

Other sources of energy, such as coal or oil, are in limited supply. One day, they may be used up. But water, this great life-giving source of energy, is never likely to run dry!

An A to Z of river facts

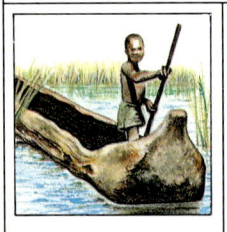

A

Amnocete
The sea lamprey larva which hatches in fresh water.

Anaconda
The world's largest snake (5 to 10 m) lives beside the waters of the tropical forests of South America.

Aquatic fauna
In all there are:
1000 species of fish
2180 species of insect
310 species of shellfish
127 species of mollusc
Aquatic animals can be classified according to their habitat: plankton is suspended in the water; nekton swims around freely; benthos lives on the bottom; neuston lives on or near the surface.

B

Butterfly fish
This flying fish is found in the tropical rivers of South America and Africa. It has broad pectoral fins which it beats together very fast until it is skimming along the surface in search of insects. Once it has gathered momentum it can rise several metres into the air.

Bayous
These are the many branches of the Mississippi which come together in the Mississippi delta. These flood plains are inhabited by descendants of the French Canadians or Acadians, who live on the water in wooden houses raised on stilts. Their chief means of transport is the canoe.

C

Current
Speed is measured

in centimetres per second:
Very slow: less than 10 cm/s
Slow: 10-25 cm/s
Average: 25-50 cm/s
Fast: 50-100 cm/s
Very fast: greater than 100 cm/s

D

Delta
The Greek for the letter D is a triangle, Delta. The Nile delta was so named because of its shape. The Mississippi, with its fingers reaching out into the Gulf of Mexico, is an example of a 'bird's foot' delta.

Drift
The force of the current causes organisms living on the river-bed to migrate downstream. The rate of drift can be as much as 1% per day. The extent of this depopulation is counteracted by newly hatched organisms and by larvae digging down into the river bed to depths of 50 cm for periods of several months on end.

E

Electric eel
An electric eel can generate enough electricity to kill a horse. When the river is in spate, the eel constructs a floating nest for its eggs. It is made of plants and other vegetable matter and measures about 1 m in diameter. The eels guard the eggs until the elvers hatch.

Eutrophic
Water becomes eutrophic when too much organic matter accumulates in it. This encourages the growth of bacteria

and algae which use up the oxygen in the water so that other organisms die.

F

Fairy shrimp
This tiny animal is found in shallow pools. It swims on its back, scuttling

under stones for safety.

G

Grand Canyon
Over millions of years, the Colorado river has carved out the steep gorges of the Grand Canyon, which is 1800 m deep in places. When the river is in spate, the level of the water can rise suddenly by as much as 40 m.

H

Hard water
is rich in calcium.

Huet
The French biologist who first defined the four main water zones (*see* p. 63).

Hydrological cycle
or **Water cycle**
The circulation of the earth's water, which evaporates into the atmosphere over the sea, falls as rain or snow and returns to the sea in rivers, and then once more to the atmosphere by evaporation.

Henley-on-Todd
A *dry* regatta held annually in Alice Springs. The crews run with fully rigged, but bottomless boats on the hard sandy bed of the river Todd, which flows only in very rainy years.

K

Klongs
Name given to the river channels of the Thailand deltas.

Kolkwitz
Biologist who discovered four distinct degrees of organic pollution in water.

L

Limicolae
Species which live on organic matter in the mud of river-beds: fish like carp, birds like the flamingo.

M

Meanders
Meanders are pronounced S-shaped loops in the course of a river. The outside banks of the bends are eroded by the river; alluvial deposits accumulate on the insides of the bends.

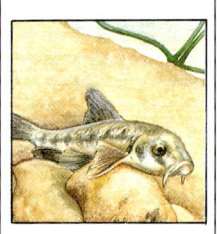

Musk-rat
This North American rodent lives in river banks. Its maze of underground burrows weakens the banks. Musk-rats breed fast. They will travel up to 20 miles in search of new homes.

Mussels
Mussels feed and breathe through siphons. Swan mussels are found on the bottoms of ponds, canals and lakes; the smaller zebra mussel clings to stones and landing stages; pearl mussels are sometimes found on the sandy bottoms of rivers, and occasionally form small pearls.

N

Niagara Falls
From an Indian word, meaning 'the strait'. Such is the force of the tumbling water that the rock at the foot of the Falls is being worn away backwards towards Lake Erie. 20000 years ago, the river flowed straight over the Falls into Lake Ontario.

O

Oued or **Wadi**
Deep, steep-sided water channels in the desert, which are usually dry, but which can fill very rapidly in periods of rain or flood.

P

Piracuru
The largest freshwater fish in the Amazon basin. The Indians use its rough skin as emery paper.

Q

Quality of water
The degree of pollution in any given river can be determined by analysing the animal life which inhabits it.

R

Rate of flow
This can be calculated in cubic metres per unit of time by measuring the volume of water flowing over a given section in a given time.

S

Sagittaria or **Arrowhead**
This plant has three types of leaves: thin trailing leaves below the surface; floating oval ones on the water; arrow-shaped leaves above the surface.

T

Toll bridges
On many modern bridges, such as Sydney Harbour Bridge, the Forth and the Severn Bridges, all bridge users are charged a toll.

V

Victoria Falls
in Zimbabwe. The Zambezi river is 1700 m wide as it plunges over the edge of a plateau to drop 122 m into a gorge only 80 m wide.

W

Waterways
In Great Britain are about 4000 kilometres of waterways being used for commercial and pleasure cruising, some 2800 kilometres for cruising alone.

About the author and the illustrator

GENEVIEVE DUMAINE, the author, is a naturalist, geologist and geophysicist. She spent some time in oceanographical research with Captain Cousteau, and then worked as a consultant in the search for undersea oil fields. She has travelled a great deal, but is now based in Paris, with a country house close to the rivers and streams of the French Massif Central.

The illustrator, BRIGITTE PARIS, was born in Tours in 1954. As a student she attended the Ecole des Arts Décoratifs in Strasbourg. She adores animals, and has 2 tortoises, 2 dogs, 1 cat, 3 rabbits, 2 guinea-pigs, 1 sparrow, 1 duck, 1 house-martin, 1 starling, some pigeons... and a hamster! She lives in Paris.

Places to go and story-books to read

Watery places in Britain to visit and explore:
SCOTLAND: The River Spey; the Lochs; the Canal Museum, Linlithgow, Lothian. NORTH OF ENGLAND: The River Ribble; the River Esk; Kielder Reservoir; the Lake District; Barton-upon-Irwell, Manchester (Barton Swing aqueduct); Leeds and Liverpool Canal (travels over 126 miles, over 91 locks). THE MIDLANDS: The River Trent; Rutland Water; the Norfolk Broads; Birmingham Canal Navigations (complex canal network on 3 levels); Foxton Locks, Leics. (staircase of 10 locks); Grand Union Canal; the Waterways Museum, Stoke Bruerne, Northants. WALES: The River Severn; the River Teifi; Llyn Briane; Taf Fechan; Pontcysylte aqueduct, Clwyd. LONDON: The River Thames; Regent's Canal and Little Venice. THE SOUTH-EAST: The River Thames; The River Arun. THE WEST COUNTRY: The River Avon; the River Exe; The River Tamar; Dundas aqueduct, Avon.

Story-books with a watery theme:
Three Men in a Boat, by Jerome K. Jerome; *Tarka the Otter*, by Henry Williamson; *The Wind in the Willows*, by Kenneth Grahame; *Minnow on the Say*, by Philippa Pearce; *Swallows and Amazons*, by Arthur Ransome; *The Fishing Party*, by William Mayne; *The Borrowers Afloat*, by Mary Norton; *The River at Green Knowe*, by Lucy Boston; *The Voyage of the QV66*, by Penelope Lively; *The Short Voyage of the Albert Ross*, by Jan Mark; *The Barge Children*, by Helen Cresswell.

Other books in the *Discoverers* series:

Discovering Nature:
**Spring
Summer
Autumn
Winter
Flowers
The Book of the Sky**

Discovering Animals:
Your Cat

Discovering History:
**Clothes through the Ages
Uniforms through the Ages
Ships and Seafarers
The Book of Inventions and Discoveries**

Discovering Art:
Painting and Painters